T0098604

FUND YOUR BOOK

FUND YOUR BOOK

5 STEPS TO FORM POWERFUL FUNDING PARTNERSHIPS

JACQUI PRETTY

NEW YORK

NASHVILLE • MELBOURNE • VANCOUVER

FUND YOUR BOOK
5 STEPS TO FORM POWERFUL FUNDING PARTNERSHIPS

© 2018 **JACQUI PRETTY**

Published in New York, New York, by Morgan James Publishing. Morgan James is a trademark of Morgan James, LLC. www.MorganJamesPublishing.com

The Morgan James Speakers Group can bring authors to your live event. For more information or to book an event visit The Morgan James Speakers Group at www.TheMorganJamesSpeakersGroup.com.

ISBN 978-1-68350-655-3 paperback
ISBN 978-1-68350-656-0 eBook
Library of Congress Control Number: 2017910176

Cover Design by:
Rachel Lopez
www.r2cdesign.com

In an effort to support local communities, raise awareness and funds, Morgan James Publishing donates a percentage of all book sales for the life of each book to Habitat for Humanity Peninsula and Greater Williamsburg.

Get involved today! Visit
www.MorganJamesBuilds.com

CONTENTS

What if you could raise $10,000+ for your book?   1

    Where most entrepreneurs go wrong   3

The power of partnerships   5

The 2 ways partners can fund your book   13

    Strategy 1: Sell your book before it exists   13

    Strategy 2: Sell advertising in your book   16

How to create successful book funding partnerships   19

    Step 1: Find potential partners   21

        1. Who shares your market?   21

        2. Who shares your values?   24

        Exercise: Brainstorm potential partners   25

    Step 2: Frontload the work   26

        1. Build your credibility and profile   27

        2. Build the relationship with your partners   34

    Step 3: Involve your partners in your book   41

Step 4: Pitch for funds   44

    1. Create your investment options   46

    2. Make the pitch   49

    3. Follow up!   52

Step 5: Keep them in the loop   53

Thank you!   57

Meet the author   59

Ready to write your awesome book?   61

WHAT IF YOU COULD RAISE $10,000+ FOR YOUR BOOK?

You've almost finished your draft and you start shopping around for publishing quotes.

One editor quotes $1,200 and another quotes $5,000. One designer will charge $500, while another charges $2,000. And then you approach an end-to-end publishing company who will charge $12,000 for the lot—editing, design, eBook, printing and distribution.

Regardless of where your suppliers sit, self-publishing a high-quality business book isn't cheap, with quotes ranging anywhere from **$3,000 to $15,000**+.

And yes, you *know* that the book is an investment. You know that the **purpose of your book isn't to make a profit by selling books** for

$25 apiece. If you're like most of my clients, you're writing a book to:

- Build your credibility
- Connect with influencers and the media
- Generate leads
- Presell potential clients
- Charge higher rates

In other words, the purpose of your book is to create *business opportunities*.

"For me, one of the key things was getting my philosophy on the book right, and that is about leveraging your whole business. We're not in the business of writing and selling books; we're using the book for a broader purpose. As long as you're covering the cost of the books through the number of sales you are making, I'd rather be getting more books out there, because I think that is the longer-term objective."

– Geoff Green, author of *The Smart Business Exit: Getting Rewarded for Your Blood, Sweat and Tears*

But up to $15,000 to get published is a huge financial hit—especially if you're in your first few years of business.

Where most entrepreneurs go wrong

If you're like most entrepreneurs, you find a way to make it happen:

 You put it on your credit card, saying, 'I'll pay it back when business picks up. After all, this book's going to bring in a flood of new clients!' All the while, you're paying 21% interest on those borrowed funds—for a book that cost $10,000, that's an extra $2,100 in interest!

 You take the money out of the business, cutting back on expenses for a few months to get enough cash together. The problem? In most businesses the easiest expense to cut is *you*—this means months without a salary, and still having to figure out how to pay the mortgage.

You put off publishing your book until you get the funds together. Unfortunately, when an entrepreneur puts off publishing their book, they're unlikely to finish at all. I have one client who had his book edited *three years ago*, and it's still not in print.

But what if you could cover the costs of publishing *before* you went to print? And, at the same time, what if you could supercharge your marketing, helping hundreds of your books get into the hands of your ideal clients?

In this proven, step-by-step guide, I'll show you how to do just that by leveraging **your most powerful business asset**—partnerships.

The best thing is that this method works:

- Even if you don't have an email list of 10,000+ subscribers
- Even if you don't have a well-known brand and instantly recognisable logo
- Even if you don't have the money for expensive advertising campaigns

Let's get started!

THE POWER OF PARTNERSHIPS

Many of us imagine entrepreneurs as solitary creatures—the insanely successful ones speak from a stage under the worship of adoring fans, while those who are just getting started work from home on a laptop while wearing pyjamas.

And the rest of us? Whether you're a solopreneur or have a team, and whether you work from home or from an office, shop or factory, it can still be isolating.

After all, the business is your baby.

You are the one who comes up with the new ideas.

You are the one cold-calling potential clients.

You are the one managing staff and freelancers.

And *you* are the one who has to find a solution when something goes wrong.

It's no wonder that so many of us try to 'go it alone' when writing a book!

Yet there are a range of benefits in teaming up with other entrepreneurs and organisations that share your values and have access to resources you can't reach on your own.

Just some of the benefits of partnerships include:

 Build your reputation. Connecting with a more established brand lends you some of that brand's credibility, which you can cash in on during sales calls or when pitching for speaking opportunities.

 Extend your reach. One thing most small business owners struggle with is reach—we spend hours on Facebook, Twitter and LinkedIn trying to increase our following. We write blog post after blog post hoping it will grow our email list. Yet often the payoff isn't proportionate to the effort you put in. Partnering with a larger organisation can give you instant access to a database of *tens, if not hundreds, of thousands.*

Create joint products and packages. Often you and your partners will have complementary skills, where each of you offers one piece of the puzzle your clients need to put together to achieve their goals (e.g. a nutritionist tackles the diet piece of the weight-loss puzzle, while a personal trainer tackles the exercise piece). By joining forces, you can create complete and remarkable solutions for your clients, which can lead to exponential returns.

Access other influencers. When it comes to the key players in any industry, there is often a small group of people or companies who are getting the most opportunities, recognition and success. The great thing about this is that they often know each other, and when you partner with one, you can get access to the rest of that inner circle.

Access more resources. Maybe there's a product or service you've been wanting to invest in for some time that you *know* will grow your business. If your partner is also interested in the same resources, you could pool funds to increase your buying power. A common example of this is coworking spaces—many entrepreneurs can't justify the overheads that come with an office, so a coworking membership gives them access to a desk in a shared space and the overheads are shared by the members.

 Increase your knowledge. Great partners are often doing great things, and building an ongoing relationship with those partners means you get to be a part of this journey. You can see what happens behind the scenes in a new product launch or marketing campaign, and apply those learnings to your own business.

Boost your profits. Yes, for the moment you're looking for someone to fund your book, but what about in future? The right partnership could lead to opportunities to be an affiliate, a keynote speaker or a consultant, all of which can add nicely to your bottom line.

And, of course, you can access thousands of dollars to offset your publishing investment.

 "For a lot of people, publishing a book means you get hit with a lot of expense within a relatively short period of time, so you effectively end up with all these books and you need to figure out how you get back some money on them quickly. Being able to sell a chunk of them upfront was good because it defrayed some costs pretty quickly."

– Geoff Green, author of *The Smart Business Exit: Getting Rewarded for Your Blood, Sweat and Tears*

Beyond the financial benefits, though, other benefits of book funding partnerships include:

- Increased credibility as an author
- The ability to leverage the partnership to distribute your book to more of your target market
- The ability to work together on future projects

"If you're clever about achieving the right partnership, then you're able to leverage that sponsorship to get the book out to more people."

– Kate Christie, author of *Me Time: The Professional Woman's Guide to Finding 30 Guilt-Free Hours a Month*

"I've just come off seven presentations around Australia in four weeks, and every single person at those events got a book. Every single one of those events was hosted by a partner and the books were bought by the partner, which means I'm not actively having to promote my book."

– Carolyn Dean, author of *Fully Booked: Dental Marketing Secrets for a Full Appointment Book*

"My sponsors have also mentioned how we could work together in future—something I wasn't prepared for at this stage as the book isn't yet published!"

– Andrea Doyle, author of *From Conflict to Consensus: Managing Workplace Conflict Well*

And the best thing is that you *don't need to be a world-famous expert or to have a huge email list* to find partners for your book!

Let's look at the entrepreneurs I interviewed for this guide—Kate Christie, Carolyn Dean, Andrea Doyle, Geoff Green and Tamara Simon.

Have you heard of them? Probably not.

That's exactly why I wanted to speak to them.

Sure, it would be easy for a CEO of one of the big four accounting firms to find corporate sponsors for his book—he's the head of a brand that thousands are scrambling to be associated with.

What I want to demonstrate in this guide is that it's possible for *you* to find funding for your book.

How do I know this? Because even though the entrepreneurs I interviewed didn't have tens of thousands of people on their email lists or a global reach, each of them raised **from $1,000 to $20,000+ for their books**.

So how do you actually do it?

Let's move on to the two common ways partners can fund your book.

THE TWO WAYS PARTNERS CAN FUND YOUR BOOK

While the ways you can fund your book will be as varied as the partners you approach, most strategies fall into two groups—bulk presales and sponsorships.

Strategy 1: Sell your book before it exists

Preselling books is a strategy that has been used by traditional publishing houses and self-publishers for years to help build buzz about a book and ensure it has a successful launch.

As a self-publisher, an added benefit is that it helps cover your publishing costs—once you take off the cost of printing and posting the copies you sell, the rest can be used for expenses like editing, design, marketing and more.

To work out how many books you need to sell to cover your costs, use this formula:

Publishing costs / (Book RRP—per-unit print cost—per-unit postage cost) = required presales

---

For instance, if I was spending $10,000 to publish my book, was selling it for $25 and knew it would cost $5 to print each copy and another $5 to post each copy, I would need to presell 667 copies. (Technically I'd need to sell 666.67, but I don't think anyone would buy two thirds of a book, so let's round up.)

$10,000 / ($25—$5—$5) = 667

Is this doable? Yes, but to do it you'll need to run a very strong marketing campaign involving a large list of potential buyers (either your own list or one that someone else is willing to share with you).

I had neither of these elements. My marketing campaign involved asking people in my network to spread the word to their networks (about 45 of them got back to me and fewer than 10 actually shared the landing page on social media. Note to self: provide juicy incentives next time). I also shared the landing page on my own social profiles, told my email list about it (then I had a grand total of 101 subscribers) and ran a Facebook ads campaign.

How many books did I sell?

11.

Clearly I'm not an expert in this area.

Fortunately I was lucky enough to speak to two authors who were much more successful.

Geoff Green, author of *The Smart Business Exit: Getting Rewarded for Your Blood, Sweat and Tears* presold 350 books at $32.95 each, adding up to over $11,500 and covering his initial print run of 1,000 books.

"The key presale for me was through my strategic alliance with a local law firm. I have a very close relationship with their private advisory area and we do a lot of work together. So for them it was a very natural opportunity to be able to push the book out to a wide network of their clients and contacts, including private business owners, accountants, wealth managers, and so on. This led to an order from them for 300 books, which covered the cost of my initial print run."

– Geoff Green, author of *The Smart Business Exit: Getting Rewarded for Your Blood, Sweat and Tears*

Meanwhile Carolyn Dean, author of *Fully Booked: Dental Marketing Secrets for a Full Appointment Book*, presold 750 copies of her $29.95 book.

"The reason that I was able to presell was because I had really good partnerships. I ended up selling 500 copies to one partner, 200 to another partner, and 50 to another. So I sold 750 books before I launched. And part of the partnership conversations with them was that they would help me launch and promote the book."

– Carolyn Dean, author of *Fully Booked: Dental Marketing Secrets for a Full Appointment Book*

Strategy 2: Sell advertising in your book

Advertising/sponsorship is when you give other businesses access to your market in exchange for a financial contribution towards your publishing costs.

This might include advertising in the back of your book, sharing their products with your email list, mentioning them from stage when you're running an event or giving a keynote, or including their logo in your marketing.

How much can you expect to get? Depending on how appealing your offer is, it can range from a few hundred dollars to several thousand—founder of Time Stylers and author of *Me Time*, Kate Christie, had one corporate sponsor cover the entire cost of her first book!

"I had one professional service firm that was interested in sponsoring me. In exchange for covering the cost of the printing, they would get branding on one side of my bookmark. But they've also gotten a lot of brand loyalty from me. Even though the initial print run is finished, I still get that same bookmark printed because they did me a really good turn. Now that my book's going out and I'm getting more coverage, it's a nice thing for me to do for them."

– Kate Christie, author of *Me Time: The Professional Woman's Guide to Finding 30 Guilt-Free Hours a Month*

Andrea Doyle, author of the upcoming book *From Conflict to Consensus: Managing Workplace Conflict Well*, had a sponsor offer to cover 20% of her editing and design costs in exchange for a one-page ad in the back of her book. (Unfortunately this agreement fell through due to internal policies at the organisation.)

And Tamara Simon sold two full-page and four half-page ads in the back of her book *The Five Little RTO Pigs*, which covered her first print run of 1,000 books.

HOW TO CREATE SUCCESSFUL BOOK FUNDING PARTNERSHIPS

A ccording to Rosabeth Moss Kanter, the author of *MOVE: Putting America's Infrastructure Back in the Lead*, there are three fundamental aspects of successful partnerships:

 They must deliver benefits for both partners. This is key, and you'll see a big part of the partnership process is not only deciding what you want from the relationship, but what you can offer your partner.

They involve collaboration, rather than just being an exchange. A collaborative partnership is where both partners create new value together, rather than each partner getting something back for what they put in. Collaborative partnerships tend to lead to greater returns in the long term, rather than just an immediate payoff.

 They rely on personal connections. Most of the entrepreneurs I interviewed already had relationships with their prospective partners when they pitched them, rather than sending cold emails.

While this sounds great in theory, how can you create a collaborative partnership based on your personal connection with your partner that delivers benefits for both you and your partner?

It comes down to five steps:

1. **Find potential partners**
2. **Frontload the work**
3. **Involve your partners in your book**

4. **Pitch for funds**
5. **Keep them in the loop**

Step 1: Find potential partners

Unsurprisingly, the first step of the process is finding potential partners to approach!

This involves asking two questions: who shares your market and who shares your values?

It's only by addressing both of these criteria that you'll find a partner who is able to deliver a real business benefit (meaning, sending more clients to your business) and who you want to work with in the long term (which paves the way for future opportunities to help each other).

1. Who shares your market?

When brainstorming people and organisations who might like to help fund your book, the best place to start is with people who share your target market but who aren't direct competitors with your product or service.

In Kate's case, her first book was about smart time management for busy women, so she focused on brands, products and services that would make their lives easier and would help them manage their time smarter. The organisation she eventually partnered with was an organisation that provides advice to big companies that saw advertising in her book as an opportunity to get their brand in front of new audiences.

Tamara was in a very tight niche, working specifically with Registered Training Organisations (RTOs), which meant she could focus on highly targeted sponsors: RTO consultants, a membership-based organisation for insurance, insurance companies that work with RTOs and companies that provide training software.

"Sponsoring is a great idea, but I think it's a great idea for a niche. If you're doing a general book, it's harder for your advertisers to add value to your book. All of my advertisers provide services specifically for RTOs—it's not just anyone."

– Tamara Simon, author of *The Five Little RTO Pigs: Helping Registered Training Organisations Build Simple, Profitable and Compliant Businesses*

On the other hand, when *Book Blueprint* first went to print, Grammar Factory offered writing workshops and editing services, so our partners could have been other businesses in the publishing space—cover designers, printers and end-to-end self-publishers. Getting broader, we could have also targeted businesses that work with entrepreneurs who are trying to grow their businesses, such as business coaches, coworking spaces and digital marketers.

Keep in mind that the more niched your business is, the easier it will be to find potential partners. First, it means you can easily hone in on the organisations targeting the same niche (this is easier to do for 'entrepreneurs who want to write a book' versus 'entrepreneurs', or 'RTOs' versus 'small businesses'). Second, it means your offer will be much more appealing for your potential partners, as it will directly target the clients they are also trying to reach.

"Niching is essential. If I had been a general marketer that looked after small businesses, would I have the biggest players in the dental industry wanting to work with me? Not a chance. It's absolutely the niche.

And the smaller the niche, the deeper you go, the more you understand the customer and their problems, and the more products you can create that help them uniquely in their space. For me, the niche is everything."

– Carolyn Dean, author of *Fully Booked: Dental Marketing Secrets for a Full Appointment Book*

2. Who shares your values?

While the business side of the partnership needs to make sense, the personal side is just as important.

Partnerships that involve shared values, a strong rapport and clear communication are more likely to transcend personal and professional storms than those that are seen as purely a transaction.

The importance of finding organisations with shared values was something all of my interviewees discussed—it isn't worth selling your soul for a few hundred, or even a few thousand, dollars.

"Integrity is key. You need to make sure that the brand you're looking to work with aligns very closely to you in terms of your values. I think you need to be very sure about what you are prepared and not prepared to do. I would urge you not to sell your soul and give up too much real estate in your book. You need to offer the partnership on terms that work for you.

So don't give away IP or compromise on your values, and don't partner with someone just because they're going to pay for the costs of the book—you have to share the same market and the same values."

– Kate Christie, author of *Me Time: The Professional Woman's Guide to Finding 30 Guilt-Free Hours a Month*

Exercise: Brainstorm potential partners

1. List 10 different categories of partners (usually different types of businesses that serve your target market).
2. For each category, list 5 specific businesses that share your values.
3. Start researching them to find one that's a match for your business!

> **Why do you need so many partners?**
>
> Unless you have already built a relationship with these businesses, you can expect far more 'nos' than 'yeses' when you approach them. Having 50+ potential partners to approach helps take the pressure off individual pitches, and also gives you the opportunity to improve your pitch to get a better result.

Step 2: Frontload the work

Regardless of their funding strategy, one of the common threads that came up in my interviews was the amount of work that came *before* pitching a partner.

'Frontloading' is a concept I learned from Ramit Sethi of I Will Teach You to Be Rich and Growth Lab. It's a concept he discusses when finding your dream job, earning more money and starting an online business. It means putting in the majority of your effort at the *beginning* of the process so that when it comes time for the job interview, asking for a raise or selling your product, your chances of success are much higher.

This concept is key when it comes to funding your self-published book, and one of the things you're about to learn is that most of the work involved in getting funding happens long before you make your pitch. (As a result, this step is the longest one in the process.)

The end result is, by the time you pitch someone about getting involved, often *they are already sold.*

How do you do it? It's important to focus on two areas: building your credibility and profile, and building a relationship with your potential partners.

1. Build your credibility and profile

When you're brainstorming potential partners, it's easy to get excited when you think about all of the books you might sell and all of the money you might make ... five sponsors at $1,000 each is $5,000! 1,000 books at $25 each is $25,000!

Before you get too carried away, remember what I said earlier about strong partnerships delivering benefits for both parties. Yes, it may be a financial windfall for you, but what can you offer *them*?

A key frontloading strategy is becoming someone your partners *want* to partner with, rather than one of dozens of pitches they receive from small business owners.

How can you do this?

By building your credibility and your profile.

Credibility

Your credibility is how trustworthy or believable you are as an expert in your field, and it naturally grows as you build your business. Some credibility markers include:

- How many years you've been in business
- How many clients you've worked with
- Whether you've worked with international clients
- Whether you've worked with any well-known brands
- The results you've achieved for your clients
- Whether you've been featured in the media
- Whether you're already affiliated with any influencers
- Whether you've spoken at any prominent events

- Whether you're a published author (hint, hint)
- Any relevant qualifications

To get started:

 List the facts for each of these points. How long have you been in business? How many clients have you worked with? Are any of them big brands? Etc.

 Gather evidence to demonstrate these points. As an author/soon-to-be author, do you have a book cover graphic and blurb you can send out? Do you have endorsements from influencers? Do you have client testimonials and case studies? (If you don't have these yet, start asking!)

Look at ways you can further build your credibility. You're already looking at connecting with influential partners, so how else can you become more credible? Do you know anyone who can introduce you to a well-known brand? Can you start submitting articles to publications in your industry? Can you subscribe to SourceBottle or HARO to be the first to hear about journalists looking for experts like you? Even if you're new to business, you can start actively working to build your credibility before your book comes out.

"My belief is you have to know what you're talking about. You really need to have the experience, you need to have the knowledge and you need to have the credibility when you talk to potential partners. We had seven years of experience in this space and runs on the board, so we were already very well-positioned and very well-known before we approached the big players."

– Carolyn Dean, author of *Fully Booked: Dental Marketing Secrets for a Full Appointment Book*

"The driving factor for my sponsors was my credibility within the sector and believing that people would buy the book because of that credibility. That would give my sponsors the opportunity to get to people that they wouldn't normally get to."

– Tamara Simon, author of *The Five Little RTO Pigs: Helping Registered Training Organisations Build Simple, Profitable and Compliant Businesses*

Profile

Credibility markers demonstrate whether or not you are truly the expert you claim to be. Your profile is how many people know about it, or your audience.

One of the benefits of partnering with larger organisations is that they can expose your business to a larger network. However, it's also important to think about what's in it for them. If you can get their business in front of thousands of new people, then that's a big reason for them to invest in you.

How big is your profile? Consider:

- How many people are on your email list?
- How many followers do you have on each of your social networks?

- How many clients have you worked with?
- How many people are you connected to through business networks?
- Are you involved in any other significant networks?

Once you know how many people you are currently reaching, the next step is to reach more people.

How?

My favourite method is publishing articles on other blogs and websites that reach my audience, like Business Insider, GrowthLab, Flying Solo, Key Person of Influence, Location180 and more. Every post puts my thoughts in front of new people and links back to my website. This leads to more traffic, more opt-ins and a larger email list!

To get started with guest posting:

1. Research blogs and websites that:
   a. Target your audience
   b. Have a bigger audience than your own blog (you can check their traffic at SimilarWeb)

    c.   Accept guest posts (an easy way to do this is to Google 'site:partnerwebsite.com guest post')

2. Review their existing content. What have they covered recently? Which posts have gotten the most comments and shares?

3. Brainstorm some article ideas that will offer something new to their audience and provide value.

4. Pitch the publication. Many will have guest post guidelines, which I recommend you follow. If they don't, check out this guest posting guide by Ramit Sethi.

If you're not a writer, or you're still working on your book and the thought of writing even more makes your stomach turn, another approach is pitching for podcast interviews. Just as with the guest posting process, you want to:

1. Research podcasts that target your audience and regularly do interviews.

2. Review past episodes to see what they find interesting.

3. Brainstorm some topics you could cover in an interview that are different from their existing content (or offer a new angle) and provide value.
4. Pitch them (you can use a similar email to the guest posting one).

You can also look at growing your audience through advertising—Facebook Ads, AdWords, LinkedIn Ads, Twitter Ads, and so on. I'm not going to go into this here because I haven't had much luck in this area, so head to Google if this is something that interests you.

2. Build the relationship with your partners

The second, more important, area of frontloading is building a relationship with your partners.

Ideally, pitching someone to help you promote or fund your book shouldn't be the first point of contact. Instead, partnerships should be a long-term approach where you should already be providing some value to your potential partners before you ask for anything from them.

Geoff Green involved a number of colleagues in his book, who gave feedback and wrote testimonials and endorsements. Some included Alan Kohler, the founder of Eureka Report and Business Spectator; Dr Tom McKaskill, serial entrepreneur and the author of Ultimate Exits; John Warrillow, the author of Built to Sell; Daniel Priestley, the author of Become a Key *Person of Influence*; and Andrew Griffiths, Australia's #1 Small Business and Entrepreneurial Author.

The common thread in all of these relationships was that he had been working with these colleagues long before his book came out. He met Andrew and Daniel through the Key Person of Influence coaching program, and had known John, Tom and Alan for years (though he mentioned that approaching Alan to do the foreword was still a bit daunting!).

 "I just gradually got to know John better and better over a two or three year period. If I'd just written to him out of the blue and said, 'I love your book Built to Sell and could you write a testimonial for my book?' that wouldn't have landed at all.

It was the fact that I found a few things that I could potentially help him with that built up the relationship bit by bit to the point where it was not

> unnatural for me to say, 'Would you mind writing a testimonial for my book?'"

– Geoff Green, author of *The Smart Business Exit: Getting Rewarded for Your Blood, Sweat and Tears*

So how can you build the relationship with an influencer?

The first step is making them aware that you exist. The method will vary depending on who you're approaching, but some ideas include:

The informal approach. Directly reach out for a coffee or chat over Skype, explaining what you do and why you'd like to connect with them. (This probably won't work for larger players.)

The stealth approach. Find ways to get on their radar without them knowing that you're seeking them out. In the real world, this might be going to an event they're hosting or attending, while online this might be commenting on their social media posts or blog.

The value-adding approach. Think of how you can add value to them. This might include making an introduction, responding to a question they have, suggesting a solution to a problem they have or, my personal favourite, offering to write a guest post. If you already have a large following of your own or regularly contribute to a major publication, you could also offer to interview them.

 The promotional approach. Market directly to your potential partners to make them aware of who you are and what you do. This is how Carolyn Dean got in front of some of the largest organisations in Australia's dental industry.

"We realised that for us to find and market to every single dentist in Australia would be very hard. But if we marketed to the people who owned that audience, then that would be a much easier mode of attack. So for a good couple of years, all of our marketing dollars actually went

> on promoting ourselves to the key players within the industry. And it's paid off hugely, because the people who work with dentists know that they need help with their marketing, and now we are the people to talk to when they need that help."

– Carolyn Dean, author of *Fully Booked: Dental Marketing Secrets for a Full Appointment Book*

Once your potential partner knows who you are, the next step is adding value. This might include:

 Reviews/testimonials. If you've used a product or service of theirs and have experienced a great result, consider leaving a testimonial—we all like to hear nice things about our work (Grammar Factory clients, consider this a not-so-subtle hint).

 Sharing information of interest. If you find an article or another piece of information that will interest them, share it with them—it's a nice way to add a little value while staying on their radar.

Help with their marketing. If they are doing great work that you believe in, offer to help promote it on social media and to your email list. Like reviews, shares are also appreciated.

 Help them create content. If your prospective partner has a strong online presence, they probably struggle to create content on a regular basis. You can help this by guest posting, connecting them with other bloggers who might be a match, and conducting more interviews.

 "The major driver for a lot of our partners is the search for quality content. Because we've been blogging and publishing on LinkedIn a lot, we already have a lot of good content that's relevant to their marketplace. This then provides a really good avenue to say, 'By the way, you can purchase a copy of my book as well.'"

– Geoff Green, author of *The Smart Business Exit: Getting Rewarded for Your Blood, Sweat and Tears*

Look for shared opportunities. Yes, in future you want to pitch your partners about funding your book, but are there any opportunities to collaborate *now*? If you share the same market, you could create a shared product, market it to your shared lists and split the profits. Or you could join forces and run an event together.

> "Our standard partner needs a dentist to be successful in business. And to achieve that, the dentist needs help with their marketing and their business. So we offered a variety of solutions, reports, surveys and assessments to our partners or to their clients, or gifts that their clients would get key benefits from."

– Carolyn Dean, author of *Fully Booked: Dental Marketing Secrets for a Full Appointment Book*

Ultimately, your partners are another market you want to attract. Just like your ideal clients, you need to understand their challenges and what they want to achieve—it's only then that you'll be able to add value.

> "When you're talking to a partner, you absolutely need to know who they are, what you can offer, what the clients need, and what the partners need. Because you've only got one chance to make a really good impression when you're talking to the big guys."
>
> – Carolyn Dean, author of *Fully Booked: Dental Marketing Secrets for a Full Appointment Book*

Step 3: Involve your partners in your book

You've built a relationship with your partners and your book is in production. Now it's time to get them involved.

If you've been in regular communication with your partners, they should already know that you're working on a book (if they don't, let them know ASAP!). One way to help warm them up to the idea of sponsoring or bulk presales is by involving them in the book itself.

How can you get them involved? Some ideas include:

Interview them for comments in the book. There's a clear incentive here as being able to say they were quoted in your book builds their credibility. It also helps you generate content and gives you the chance to flag that you might have more opportunities for them to be involved down the track.

Ask if you can quote their published content. If one or more of your partners is very busy and important, you can approach them about quoting them in the book. This alerts them to the fact that you're writing a book and allows them to be involved, but it doesn't require a lot of their time to take part.

Ask them to review your content. Having your partners review your content (either the full book or relevant chapters) helps create a sense of ownership in the book for them, which makes them more likely to support the book going forward.

 Ask for endorsements. Endorsements go a long way to boosting the credibility of your book, especially if your market is already familiar with the people who endorse you. And, once again, it's a way to get your partners involved.

 "I did a lot of consultation in the writing process. I had a lot of people looking at drafts and had a love of conversations with people in the industry. So there are a lot of people who feel some ownership in my book because I talked to them a lot, which built up a lot of goodwill around the book and supported the book going forward."

– Geoff Green, author of *The Smart Business Exit: Getting Rewarded for Your Blood, Sweat and Tears*

Having your partners involved throughout the writing process will make the transition towards asking for funds much more natural. In fact, they may even ask *you* how they can get involved!

Step 4: Pitch for funds

How you make your pitch will depend on whether you already have a relationship with your potential partners.

If you've followed the advice in this guide, then you should have a relationship, which means your pitch can be relatively informal—you can discuss options for sponsoring your book and come to a win-win arrangement over a coffee or Skype.

Once again, the key is knowing your partners—what are they trying to achieve, and how will sponsoring or pre-ordering your book help them achieve that goal?

Carolyn Dean timed her book launch to coincide with the largest dental marketing expo in Australia, which is run every two years. The first reason for this was for maximum exposure to her market, and the second was because she knew at least one of her partners would need gifts for the expo.

The result? One of her partners ordered 500 copies they could use as gifts.

"I knew that one of our partners offered gifts at the big expos, and a book is a great gift. I also knew the biannual conference was coming up and I knew what the big guys would offer, so I knew that the book could be a really good gift for purchase."

– Carolyn Dean, author of *Fully Booked: Dental Marketing Secrets for a Full Appointment Book*

Meanwhile, Andrea Doyle reached out to a former employer for sponsorship, knowing that a training program they offered would be a perfect match for the readers of her book. The way she positioned it was that a single sale would make back her partner's investment.

"I wanted to make it easy for them to see the benefits. Their ROI would be easy to attain—if only one person who reads my book does their course, they have nearly doubled their investment."

– Andrea Doyle, author of *From Conflict to Consensus: Managing Workplace Conflict Well*

But what if you aren't sure what your partners would like, or they don't know what they want, or (heaven forbid) you're making a cold pitch? Then it's a good idea to create some investment options for them to choose from.

1. Create your investment options

When creating your investment options, you need to consider:

- The levels of investment available
- What your partners will get at each level
- An outline of the benefits for them

For instance, you might offer three investment options—gold, silver and bronze—where sponsors at each level receive different levels of marketing exposure, as demonstrated in the following table.

	Bronze	Silver	Gold
Full page ad in the back of the book	Y	Y	Y
Banner & exhibit booth at book launch	Y	Y	Y
Business link & logo on book website/landing page	Y	Y	Y
Business link & logo on bookmark		Y	Y
Industry exclusivity		Y	Y
Banner & exhibit booth at speaking engagements		Y	Y
Promotional material shared at trade shows		Y	Y
Be interviewed by the author and have comments included in book			Y
Product placement within book content			Y
Author keynote speech/ workshop			Y
Investment	$XXXX	$XXXX	$XXXX

Keep in mind that what you offer needs to be enticing to your partners. For instance, a wedding dress designer may regularly get a booth at local wedding expos, and could offer to include partner brochures and business cards in the free goodie bag they hand out. However, offering to share promotional material at an expo or trade show would be less appealing to someone who works largely in the online space and doesn't have physical marketing material.

Similarly, including your partners' links and logos in your email marketing may be appealing if you already have 10,000+ people on that list, but if you only have a few hundred, that will be less of an incentive for them to invest.

At this stage it's also important to consider the investment your partners will be making. There are a few options here—usually a flat fee, buying a certain number of books, or a combination of the two.

My preference would be asking your sponsors to buy a certain number of books (let's say 100 books for your bronze tier, 200 for your silver tier and 300 for your gold tier).

Why?

Although you won't have as much free cash (remember, you need to pay for printing and postage for the books they order), this has the added benefit of distribution—rather than simply getting funding to put towards your book, you could have partners who have the *exact same target market as you* handing out hundreds of your books to your ideal clients. Suddenly your book marketing is happening by itself!

Keep in mind that these tiers are a starting point. Their only role is to open a conversation, so be willing to negotiate with your partners to find a win-win arrangement.

2. Make the pitch

Now that you have your investment options in place, it's time to make your pitch!

If you have already spoken to your partners and they have verbally agreed to sponsor your book or make a large order, then this step might just involve writing an email to confirm the details.

If this is your initial approach about funding, but there is an existing relationship and they are aware you are writing a book, you can get started with the following template:

Hi *[Name]*,

I hope you're well.

As you know, I have been building my business **[outline what your business does]**. In **[month] [year]** I will be publishing my first book, **[book title]**, which is targeted at **[describe target market]**.

[Describe connection between your business and your sponsor's business—do you share the same target market? Do they have a product or service that complements your book's main message?]

As a result, I would like to offer you the opportunity to promote **[sponsor's business name]** as part of my book's marketing campaign.

[Outline sponsorship options and investment levels.]

[If appropriate, explain how long it will take for your sponsors to make back their investment.]

[Outline how you will be marketing your book. This may include existing marketing— the size of your email list or database, whether you've had any media appearances, and whether you've had any speaking engagements—as well as future marketing plans.]

> *If you would like to discuss this further, I am available to make a time to chat **[in person/over the phone/via Skype]**.*
>
> *I look forward to hearing from you,*
> ***[Your name]***

if you *don't* have an existing relationship with your potential partner, then you can use a similar template to the one above, but you will need to give a bit more background before you launch into your offer, including:

- **Explaining how you learnt about their business:** Were you introduced to them by a mutual connection? Have you been reading their blog or enjoying their podcast? Did you attend one of their events?
- **Introducing yourself and your business:** What do you do and who do you work with? What's the title of your book and when will it come out?
- **Explaining the link between your two businesses:** Do you have the same target

market? Do you share the same values? Do you have complementary products or services?

3. Follow up!

Finally, remember that your partners are probably very busy running their own businesses, so don't panic if you don't hear back from them straight away. If you don't hear anything in seven days, resend your original email with the following message at the beginning:

Hi *[Name]*,

*I just wanted to follow up to make sure you got the email below. **[If you were connected by a mutual contact, remind them of this connection and who you are here.]***

Let me know if you had any questions.

Thanks,

[Your name]

Most people don't take the time to follow up, which means the potential partners you are contacting are likely to take notice when you do.

Step 5: Keep them in the loop

You will probably reach out to your partners months before your book is released, so keep them posted throughout the process.

For sponsors, your initial communication with them will focus on getting the collateral you need from them—this will include logos, headshots, marketing copy, and designs to include in your book or in its marketing material. For those ordering in bulk, it will involve invoicing them for the books.

However, after this it's easy to fall into radio silence, leaving them wondering exactly what's happening.

Instead, consider writing a monthly partner email with an update on what's happening with your book. This might include:

- **How the content is progressing:** Where are you up to with your draft? Have you received feedback from trial readers? Do you have some reader testimonials you can share with your sponsors?
- **The publishing process:** Is your book being edited? Do you have cover design

concepts you can share? Can you send them a photo of you posing with a proof copy of your book?

- **Your marketing campaign:** Your book marketing campaign should start long before your book comes out. So keep your sponsors posted on what you're up to— have you been featured in the media? Did you have another speaking engagement? Have you presold some more books? This will help reassure them that your book will be putting their business in front of their target market.

Keep it personal!

Remember that one of the three elements of successful partnerships is having a personal connection, so keep things personal. This means your monthly partner email is not a bulk email to all of your partners, but one that you write to each of them.

For extra points, keep note of any interesting tidbits, projects they have in progress, events they have coming up or goals they are working toward during your conversations—in your monthly email, you can start by asking for an update on these.

This will add a personal touch and open up a potential conversation, unlike a one-way update on how you and your book are doing.

THANK YOU!

I'd like to say a big thank you to Kate Christie, Carolyn Dean, Andrea Doyle, Geoff Green and Tamara Simon, who generously let me pick their brains for this article. You can learn more about their books and businesses at:

- Kate Christie, author of *Me Time: The Professional Woman's Guide to Finding 30 Guilt-Free Hours a Month* and founder of Time Stylers
- Carolyn Dean, author of *Fully Booked: Dental Marketing Secrets for a Full Appointment Book* and founder of My Dental Marketing
- Andrea Doyle, author of *From Conflict to Consensus: Managing Workplace Conflict Well* and founder of Doyle Solutions

- Geoff Green, author of *The Smart Business Exit: Getting Rewarded for Your Blood, Sweat and Tears* and founder of The Smart Business Exit
- Tamara Simon, author of *The Five Little RTO Pigs: Helping Registered Training Organisations Build Simple, Profitable and Compliant Businesses* and founder of Business Scene Investigation

Hi there! I'm Jacqui, the author of the award-winning book *Book Blueprint: How any entrepreneur can write an awesome book* and the founder of Grammar Factory, a publishing company that turns entrepreneurs into authors.

Since the launch of Grammar Factory in 2013, my team and I have worked with over 100 entrepreneurs across a range of industries—including business, finance, health and wellness, travel, marketing, property, hospitality, law, photography, personal development and more.

Although our clients have a mountain of knowledge to share, I've found there are a few common stumbling blocks:

- They have no idea what to write a book about, or have too many ideas and don't know which one's the best match for their business goals.
- They aren't writers and struggle with the writing process, often doing a big brain dump that needs significant work (and costs significant dollars) in the editing process, or giving up and not finishing at all.
- They put so much focus and energy into just getting the book finished that they don't think about what happens *next*, leaving them with a big debt and hundreds, *even thousands*, of books they don't know what to do with.

My mission is to solve these problems by creating a systematic approach to the writing, publishing and leveraging processes that *anyone* can follow to achieve success.

How about you? Where are you in the writing and publishing process, and what's your number one struggle right now?

Let me know at jacqui@grammarfactory.com—I read every email.

READY TO WRITE YOUR AWESOME BOOK?

A book can turn you into an industry celebrity overnight. Just think—speaking engagements, media opportunities, strategic partnerships and new clients, which are all the result of your paperback.

Essentially, a book is the ultimate business card.

But only if you do it right.

While the idea of putting pen to paper (or fingers to keyboard) is getting more popular in entrepreneurial circles, there's an elephant in the room...

Most books by entrepreneurs aren't very good. In fact, you could say they suck. Sure, they have flashy covers and catchy titles, but when you open them up, more often than not **it's all sizzle and no steak**.

If you've been thinking about just pumping out another shallow business book, or recording a few hours of fluffy personal development musings for your VA to transcribe, you'll find yourself **wasting thousands of dollars and hundreds of hours** to produce a book that won't make *any* tangible difference to your business.

Fortunately, we can help. My team and I have put together **an ultimate resource portal** that hundreds of entrepreneurs have already used to find the right book idea, beat writer's block, get published and leverage their book to double their revenue.

What will you get?

- **How a book can transform your business**—the 10 reasons every entrepreneur should get published
- **Interviews from bestselling entrepreneurs turned authors**, one of whom failed high school English!
- **The top 7 mistakes entrepreneurs make** when writing their books, and what you should do instead

- **The 3 keys to finding a bestselling book idea**, covered in a free download from my award-winning book, *Book Blueprint*
- A 45-minute webinar sharing our **number one strategy for writing a great book** ... FAST
- **Our streamlined 7-step process to self-publish**—no questions, worries or hiccups required
- Weekly emails to keep you motivated and hold you accountable to writing, publishing and leveraging your book to boost your business

Get instant access at grammarfactory.com/awesome-book-guide

Morgan James
Speakers Group

🔗 www.TheMorganJamesSpeakersGroup.com

We connect Morgan James published
authors with live and online events
and audiences who will benefit
from their expertise.